delicious **diet** recipes

D0338636

Main Dishes
for 1 or 2

Table of Contents

Rosemary-Garlic Scallops with Polenta

- 2 teaspoons olive oil
- 1 medium red bell pepper, sliced
- ⅓ cup chopped red onion
- 3 cloves garlic, minced
- ½ pound fresh bay scallops
- 2 teaspoons chopped fresh rosemary, plus additional for garnish
- ¼ teaspoon black pepper
- 1¼ cups fat-free reduced-sodium chicken broth
- ½ cup cornmeal
- ¼ teaspoon salt

1. Heat oil in large nonstick skillet over medium heat. Add bell pepper, onion and garlic; cook and stir 5 minutes. Add scallops, 2 teaspoons rosemary and black pepper; cook and stir 3 to 5 minutes or until scallops are opaque.

2. Meanwhile, combine broth, cornmeal and salt in small saucepan. Bring to a boil over high heat. Reduce heat to low; simmer 5 minutes or until polenta is very thick, stirring frequently. Divide polenta between 2 serving plates. Top with scallop mixture. Garnish with additional rosemary.   *Makes 2 servings*

Calories 304, **Total Fat** 8g, **Saturated Fat** 1g, **Protein** 26g, **Carbohydrate** 33g, **Cholesterol** 53mg, **Dietary Fiber** 4g, **Sodium** 731mg

Dietary Exchanges: 2 Starch, 3 Meat

Steak Diane with Cremini Mushrooms

  2 beef tenderloin steaks (4 ounces each)
  ¼ teaspoon black pepper
  ⅓ cup sliced shallots or chopped onion
  4 ounces cremini mushrooms, sliced *or* 1 (4-ounce) package sliced mixed wild mushrooms
  1½ tablespoons Worcestershire sauce
  1 tablespoon Dijon mustard

1. Spray large skillet with nonstick cooking spray; heat over medium-high heat. Add steaks; sprinkle with pepper. Cook 3 minutes per side for medium-rare or until desired doneness is reached. Remove to plate; keep warm.

2. Spray same skillet with cooking spray; heat over medium heat. Add shallots; cook and stir 2 minutes. Add mushrooms; cook and stir 3 minutes. Add Worcestershire sauce and mustard; cook and stir 1 minute.

3. Return steaks and any accumulated juices to skillet; cook until heated through, turning once. Transfer steaks to serving plates; top with mushroom mixture.   *Makes 2 servings*

Note: Serve steak with a fresh garden salad or sautéed vegetables.

Calories 239, **Total Fat** 9g, **Saturated Fat** 3g,
Protein 28g, **Carbohydrate** 10g, **Cholesterol** 70mg,
Dietary Fiber 1g, **Sodium** 302mg

Dietary Exchanges: 1 Vegetable, 4 Meat

Quinoa Stuffed Eggplant

- 1 eggplant
- ¼ cup uncooked quinoa
- ½ cup water
- 2 teaspoons olive oil
- ½ cup chopped onion
- 1 clove garlic, chopped
- 2 cups baby spinach, finely chopped
- 4 tablespoons crumbled feta cheese, divided
- Juice of 1 lemon
- Chopped fresh parsley (optional)

1. Preheat oven to 400°F. Slice eggplant in half lengthwise. Scoop out flesh, leaving ½-inch shell. Finely chop scooped out flesh and set aside. Place eggplant halves in baking dish. Bake 30 minutes. *Reduce oven temperature to 350°F.*

2. Meanwhile, place quinoa in fine-mesh strainer; rinse well under cold running water. Bring ½ cup water to a boil in small saucepan; stir in quinoa. Reduce heat to low; cover and simmer 10 to 15 minutes or until quinoa is tender and water is absorbed.

3. Heat oil in large skillet over medium-high heat. Add onion and chopped eggplant; cook and stir 10 minutes or until vegetables are browned and tender. Add garlic; cook and stir 1 minute. Remove from heat. Stir in quinoa, spinach, 2 tablespoons feta cheese and lemon juice.

4. Spoon quinoa mixture evenly into eggplant shells. Top evenly with remaining 2 tablespoons feta cheese.

5. Bake 15 minutes or until eggplant is softened and cheese is browned. Garnish with parsley.   *Makes 2 servings*

Serving Size: 1 filled eggplant half
Calories 261, **Total Fat** 10g, **Saturated Fat** 3g,
Protein 11g, **Carbohydrate** 38g, **Cholesterol** 13mg,
Dietary Fiber 13g, **Sodium** 230mg

Dietary Exchanges: 2 Starch, 1 Fat, 1 Vegetable, 1 Meat

Spicy Tuna Sushi Bowl

- **2** tablespoons low-fat mayonnaise
- **1** teaspoon sriracha* or hot chili sauce
- **3** teaspoons unseasoned rice wine vinegar, divided
- **1** tuna steak (about 6 ounces)
- **⅔** cup hot cooked brown rice
- **¼** cup diced cucumber
- **¼** ripe avocado, sliced
- Black sesame seeds (optional)

Sriracha is a Thai hot sauce and is available in Asian specialty markets.

1. Whisk mayonnaise, sriracha sauce and 1 teaspoon vinegar in small bowl. Rub tuna evenly with half of sauce. Marinate 10 minutes.

2. Meanwhile, stir remaining 2 teaspoons vinegar into rice; set aside.

3. Heat small nonstick skillet over medium-high heat. Cook tuna 2 minutes per side for medium-rare or until desired doneness is reached. Slice tuna.

4. Divide rice, cucumber, avocado and tuna slices between 2 serving bowls. Sprinkle evenly with sesame seeds, if desired. Drizzle evenly with remaining half of sauce. *Makes 2 servings*

Calories 212, **Total Fat** 5g, **Saturated Fat** 1g, **Protein** 23g, **Carbohydrate** 20g, **Cholesterol** 33mg, **Dietary Fiber** 2g, **Sodium** 238mg

Dietary Exchanges: 2 Starch, 3 Meat

Salmon Caesar Salad

- **1** (4-ounce) skinless salmon fillet
- **3** cups chopped romaine lettuce
- **1** tablespoon light creamy Caesar salad dressing
- **6** fat-free croutons
- **1** teaspoon grated Parmesan cheese

1. Spray small skillet with nonstick cooking spray; heat over medium heat. Add salmon; cook 4 minutes per side or until salmon flakes easily when tested with fork. When cool enough to handle, cut into bite-size pieces.

2. Meanwhile, combine lettuce and dressing in medium bowl; toss to coat evenly.

3. Arrange lettuce on serving plate. Top with salmon, croutons and cheese.

Makes 1 serving

Calories 263, **Total Fat** 11g, **Saturated Fat** 2g, **Protein** 26g, **Carbohydrate** 12g, **Cholesterol** 63mg, **Dietary Fiber** 3g, **Sodium** 344mg

Dietary Exchanges: ½ Starch, 1 Fat, 1 Vegetable, 3 Meat

Thai Curry Stir-Fry

½ cup fat-free reduced-sodium chicken broth

2 teaspoons cornstarch

2 teaspoons low-sodium soy sauce

1½ teaspoons curry powder

⅛ teaspoon red pepper flakes

2 cups broccoli florets

⅔ cup sliced carrots

3 green onions, sliced

2 cloves garlic, minced

1½ teaspoons olive oil

6 ounces boneless skinless chicken breasts, cut into ½-inch pieces

⅔ cup hot cooked rice

1. Whisk broth, cornstarch, soy sauce, curry powder and red pepper flakes in medium bowl until well blended; set aside.

2. Spray wok or large skillet with nonstick cooking spray; heat over medium-high heat. Add broccoli and carrots; cook and stir 1 to 2 minutes. Add green onions and garlic; cook and stir 1 minute or until vegetables are crisp-tender. Remove to large bowl.

3. Heat oil in wok over medium-high heat. Add chicken; cook and stir 2 to 3 minutes or until no longer pink. Stir broth mixture; add to wok. Cook and stir until sauce comes to a boil and thickens slightly. Return all vegetables to wok; cook and stir until heated through. Serve over rice. *Makes 2 servings*

Calories 273, **Total Fat** 6g, **Saturated Fat** 1g, **Protein** 28g, **Carbohydrate** 27g, **Cholesterol** 57mg, **Dietary Fiber** 5g, **Sodium** 308mg

Dietary Exchanges: 1 Starch, 2 Vegetable, 3 Meat

Baked Pasta Casserole

1½ cups uncooked wagon wheel or rotelle pasta

3 ounces 95% lean ground beef

2 tablespoons chopped onion

2 tablespoons chopped green bell pepper

1 clove garlic, minced

½ cup pasta sauce, any flavor

Dash black pepper

2 tablespoons shredded Italian-style cheese blend

Pepperoncini (optional)

1. Preheat oven to 350°F. Cook pasta according to package directions, omitting salt; drain.

2. Meanwhile, brown beef, onion, bell pepper and garlic 6 to 8 minutes in medium saucepan over medium-high heat, stirring to break up meat. Drain fat.

3. Stir pasta and pasta sauce into saucepan; sprinkle with pepper. Spoon mixture into 1-quart baking dish. Sprinkle with cheese.

4. Bake 15 minutes or until heated through. Serve with pepperoncini, if desired. *Makes 2 servings*

Note: To make ahead, assemble casserole as directed above through step 3. Cover and refrigerate several hours or overnight. Bake, uncovered, in preheated 350°F oven 30 minutes or until heated through.

Calories 282, **Total Fat** 7g, **Saturated Fat** 3g, **Protein** 16g, **Carbohydrate** 37g, **Cholesterol** 31mg, **Dietary Fiber** 3g, **Sodium** 368mg

Dietary Exchanges: 2 Starch, 1 Fat, 2 Vegetable, 1 Meat

South-of-the-Border Lunch Express

¼ cup chopped seeded tomato

2 tablespoons chunky salsa

2 tablespoons rinsed and drained canned black beans

2 tablespoons thawed frozen corn

⅛ teaspoon chopped fresh cilantro

⅛ teaspoon chopped garlic

Dash ground red pepper

½ cup cooked brown rice

Shredded reduced-fat Cheddar cheese (optional)

Microwave Directions

1. Combine tomato, salsa, beans, corn, cilantro, garlic and ground red pepper in large microwavable bowl. Cover with vented plastic wrap. Microwave on HIGH 1 to 1½ minutes or until heated through; stir.

2. Microwave rice in separate large microwavable bowl on HIGH 1 to 1½ minutes or until heated through. Top with tomato mixture and cheese, if desired. *Makes 1 serving*

Variation: To make this vegetarian dish even more satisfying, add pinto beans.

Calories 175, **Total Fat** 2g, **Saturated Fat** 0g, **Protein** 5g, **Carbohydrate** 35g, **Cholesterol** 0mg, **Dietary Fiber** 5g, **Sodium** 244mg

Dietary Exchanges: 2 Starch, ½ Vegetable

White Bean and Chicken Ragoût

- 2 boneless skinless chicken thighs
- 2 small carrots, cut into ½-inch pieces
- 2 medium stalks celery, cut into ½-inch pieces
- ¼ medium onion, chopped
- 1 whole bay leaf
- 1 sprig fresh parsley
- 1 clove garlic
- 1 sprig fresh thyme
- 3 black peppercorns
- 1 cup cooked cannellini beans
- 1 plum tomato, chopped
- 1 teaspoon herbes de Provence
- ½ teaspoon salt
- ⅛ teaspoon black pepper
- 1 teaspoon extra virgin olive oil
- 1 tablespoon chopped fresh parsley
- Grated peel of 1 lemon

1. Place chicken in medium saucepan; add enough water to cover. Add carrots, celery, onion, bay leaf, parsley, garlic, thyme and peppercorns. Bring to a boil over high heat; reduce heat to low. Simmer 15 to 20 minutes or until vegetables are tender.

2. Remove chicken from saucepan; let cool 5 minutes or until cool enough to handle.

3. Drain vegetables; reserve broth. Remove and discard bay leaf, parsley, garlic, thyme and peppercorns.

4. Cut chicken into bite-size pieces. Return chicken and vegetables to saucepan. Stir in beans, tomato, herbes de Provence, salt, black pepper and 1 cup reserved broth. Simmer 5 minutes.

5. Divide ragoût between 2 bowls; drizzle with oil. Sprinkle with chopped parsley and lemon peel.

Makes 2 servings

Serving Size: 1½ cups
Calories 283, **Total Fat** 6g, **Saturated Fat** 1g,
Protein 24g, **Carbohydrate** 36g, **Cholesterol** 57mg,
Dietary Fiber 10g, **Sodium** 715mg

Dietary Exchanges: 2 Starch, 3 Meat

Southwest Roasted Salmon & Corn

- 2 medium ears fresh corn, unhusked
- 1 salmon fillet (6 ounces), cut in half
- 1 tablespoon plus 1 teaspoon lime juice, divided
- 1 clove garlic, minced
- ½ teaspoon chili powder
- ¼ teaspoon ground cumin
- ¼ teaspoon dried oregano
- ⅛ teaspoon salt, divided
- ⅛ teaspoon black pepper
- 2 teaspoons margarine or butter, melted
- 2 teaspoons minced fresh cilantro

1. Pull back husks from each ear of corn, leaving attached. Discard silk. Bring husks back up over each ear. Soak corn in cold water 20 minutes.

2. Preheat oven to 400°F. Spray shallow 1-quart baking dish with nonstick cooking spray. Place salmon, skin side down, in prepared dish. Pour 1 tablespoon lime juice over fish. Marinate 15 minutes.

3. Combine garlic, chili powder, cumin, oregano, half of salt and pepper in small bowl. Pat salmon dry with paper towel; rub garlic mixture over salmon.

4. Remove corn from water. Place corn directly on oven rack. Roast 10 minutes; turn. Place salmon in baking dish next to corn. Roast 15 minutes or until fish begins to flake when tested with fork and corn is tender.

5. Combine margarine, cilantro, remaining 1 teaspoon lime juice and remaining salt in small bowl. Remove husks from corn. Brush over corn. Serve with salmon. *Makes 2 servings*

Note: Roasting corn gives it a flavor. However, it can also be cooked in boiling water. Omit steps 1 and 4. Husk the corn and place in a large pot of boiling water. Cover; remove from heat and let stand for 10 minutes. Drain and brush with cilantro butter as directed.

Calories 186, **Total Fat** 6g, **Saturated Fat** 1g,
Protein 19g, **Carbohydrate** 16g, **Cholesterol** 43mg,
Dietary Fiber 2g, **Sodium** 243mg

Dietary Exchanges: 1 Starch, 2 Meat

Apple-Cherry Glazed Pork Chops

- ¼ to ½ teaspoon dried thyme
- ⅛ teaspoon salt
- ⅛ teaspoon black pepper
- 2 boneless pork loin chops (3 ounces each), trimmed of fat
- ⅔ cup unsweetened apple juice
- ½ small apple, sliced
- 2 tablespoons sliced green onion
- 2 tablespoons dried tart cherries
- 1 tablespoon water
- 1 teaspoon cornstarch

1. Combine thyme, salt and pepper in small bowl. Rub onto both sides of pork chops.

2. Spray large skillet with cooking spray; heat over medium heat. Add pork chops; cook 3 to 5 minutes or until barely pink in center, turning once. Remove to plate; keep warm.

3. Add apple juice, apple slices, green onion and cherries to same skillet. Simmer 2 to 3 minutes or until apple and onion are tender.

4. Stir water into cornstarch in small bowl until smooth; stir into skillet. Bring to a boil; cook and stir until thickened. Spoon apple mixture over pork chops.

Makes 2 servings

Serving Size: 1 pork chop with about ½ cup apple-cherry glaze
Calories 243, **Total Fat** 8g, **Saturated Fat** 3g, **Protein** 19g, **Carbohydrate** 23g, **Cholesterol** 40mg, **Dietary Fiber** 1g, **Sodium** 191mg

Dietary Exchanges: 1 Fat, 1½ Fruit, 2 Meat

Bolognese Sauce & Penne Pasta

- 8 ounces 95% lean ground beef
- ⅓ cup chopped onion
- 1 clove garlic, minced
- 1 can (8 ounces) tomato sauce
- ⅓ cup chopped carrot
- ¼ cup water
- 2 tablespoons red wine
- 1 teaspoon Italian seasoning
- 1½ cups hot cooked penne pasta
- Chopped fresh parsley

1. Brown beef, onion and garlic 6 to 8 minutes in medium saucepan over medium-high heat, stirring to break up meat. Drain fat.

2. Add tomato sauce, carrot, water, wine and Italian seasoning; bring to a boil. Reduce heat; simmer 15 minutes.

3. Serve sauce over pasta. Sprinkle with parsley.   *Makes 2 servings*

Serving Size: ¾ cup cooked pasta with half of sauce
Calories 292, **Total Fat** 5g, **Saturated Fat** 2g,
Protein 21g, **Carbohydrate** 40g, **Cholesterol** 45mg,
Dietary Fiber 4g, **Sodium** 734mg

Dietary Exchanges: 2 Starch, 1 Vegetable, 2 Meat

Egg White Salad Cucumber Boats

- 6 hard-cooked eggs, peeled
- ⅓ cup light mayonnaise
  Juice of 1 lemon
- 1 teaspoon minced fresh dill, plus additional for garnish
- ¼ teaspoon salt
- ¼ cup finely chopped green bell pepper
- ¼ cup finely chopped red bell pepper
- 2 tablespoons finely chopped red onion
- 1 English cucumber

1. Slice eggs in half lengthwise; discard yolks. Finely grate or chop egg whites.

2. Whisk mayonnaise, lemon juice, 1 teaspoon dill and salt in medium bowl. Gently stir in egg whites, bell peppers and onion.

3. Cut cucumber in half crosswise; cut each piece in half lengthwise to make 4 equal pieces. Scoop out cucumber pieces with rounded ½ teaspoon, leaving thick shell.

4. Fill each shell evenly with egg white salad. Garnish with additional dill.

Makes 2 servings

Serving Size: 2 filled cucumber halves
Calories 175, **Total Fat** 9g, **Saturated Fat** 1g,
Protein 12g, **Carbohydrate** 11g, **Cholesterol** 6mg,
Dietary Fiber 1g, **Sodium** 756mg

Dietary Exchanges: 1½ Fat, 2 Vegetable, 1 Meat

Italian Primavera Lunch-Box Express

- 1 cup thawed frozen vegetable blend (broccoli, carrots and cauliflower)
- ¾ cup chunky garden-style pasta sauce
- ¼ teaspoon Italian seasoning
- 1 cup cooked brown rice

  Grated Parmesan cheese (optional)

Microwave Directions

1. Combine vegetables, sauce and seasoning in 1-quart microwavable bowl. Cover with vented plastic wrap. Microwave on HIGH 1 to 1½ minutes or until heated through; stir.

2. Microwave rice on HIGH 1 to 1½ minutes or until heated through. Top with vegetable mixture and cheese, if desired. *Makes 1 serving*

Calories 197, **Total Fat** 2g, **Saturated Fat** 1g, **Protein** 5g, **Carbohydrate** 39g, **Cholesterol** 0mg, **Dietary Fiber** 5g, **Sodium** 379mg

Dietary Exchanges: 2 Starch, 2 Vegetable